TREASURES TO FIND

BY DALE MCNEVIN

THE ACORN PRESS
CHARLOTTETOWN
2011

To my daughter Anne, through thick and thin.

- DM

Critter illustrations (pages 5 and 21) by Alyssa Murphy

ISBN 978-1-894838-55-9

ACORNPRESS

P.O. Box 22024
Charlottetown, Prince Edward Island
C1A 9J2
acornpresscanada.com

Printed and Bound in Canada
Cover and interior design by Matt Reid
Edited by Sherie Hodds

Library and Archives Canada Cataloguing in Publication
McNevin, Dale, 1945-
Treasures to find / Dale McNevin.
ISBN 978-1-894838-55-9

I. Title.
PS8625.N58T74 2011 jC813'.6 C2011-902599-X

Canada

Canada Council for the Arts / Conseil des Arts du Canada

The publisher acknowledges the support of the Government of Canada through the Canada Book Fund of the Department of Canadian Heritage and the Canada Council for the Arts Block Grant Program.

PEI Literacy Alliance

The PEI Literacy Alliance advances literacy for the people of PEI.

I want to read a book,
but I don't know what to read.

Will it be about pirates or princesses, wizards or kings

little girls and little boys,
fortune tellers and circus rings?

Will it be about how to be big,
or how to grow tall,

or maybe a book about
being quite small?

Will it be about falling
in love or in clover,
or rolling downhill,
twirling over and over?

Will it be about
dragon kites,
or carnival sights,
things that
light up the sky,

a jewel in a crown,
a fairy’s gown,
or a book that will
just answer why?

Will it be about
hills to climb,
treasures to find,
fiddles, stories and songs,

a fearless young knight
riding brave to the fight,
or a lion, proud and strong?

Will it be about dancing
through fields of my dreams,
traveling to places that
I’ve never been?

A brand new book
and a comfy chair,
a rainy day with time to spare.

I want to read a book.